by Nancy and Randall Faber

THE BASIC PIANO METHOD

CONTENTS

About the "Sightreading Stocking Stuffers"

A student's enthusiasm for learning Christmas music can become an opportunity to create enthusiasm for sightreading. In this book, each Christmas song is presented with short melodies, called "Sightreading Stocking Stuffers."

The "Sightreading Stocking Stuffers" are **melodic variations** of the carol being studied. Through repetition of familiar rhythmic and melodic patterns, the student begins to build a visual and aural musical vocabulary.

The "stocking stuffers" provide opportunity for transposition, reinforcing theory, and musicianship skills.

The student should sightread one "stocking stuffer" a day while learning the Christmas song. Or, the stocking stuffers can be used as sightreading during the lesson itself.

The teacher may wish to tell the student:

> **Sightreading means "reading music at first sight."**
>
> When sightreading, music is not practiced over and over. Instead, it is only played several times with the highest concentration.

The following **3 C's** may help the student with sightreading:

CORRECT HAND POSITION
Find the correct starting note for each hand.
Scan the music for rhythmic and melodic patterns.

COUNT - OFF
Set a steady tempo by counting one "free" measure
before starting to play.

CONCENTRATE
Focus your eyes on the music, carefully reading the intervals.
Remember to keep your eyes moving ahead!

FF12

Note to Teacher: This page reviews theory concepts in the major keys of C, G, F, and D and the minor keys of Am and Dm. This will help prepare the student for the carols and sightreading that follow.

Stuffing the Stockings

Draw a line connecting each "gift" to the correct stocking.

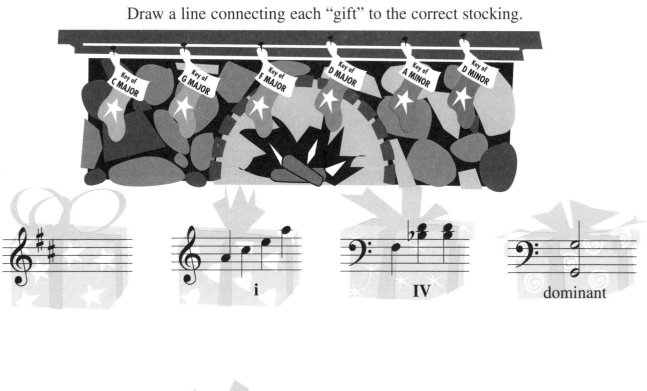

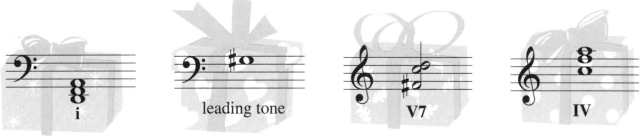

Silent Night

Words by Joseph Mohr
Music by Franz Grüber

Sightread one "stocking stuffer" a day while learning the carol. Your teacher may also ask you to transpose.

Circle the stocking after sightreading!

("variations" for sightreading)

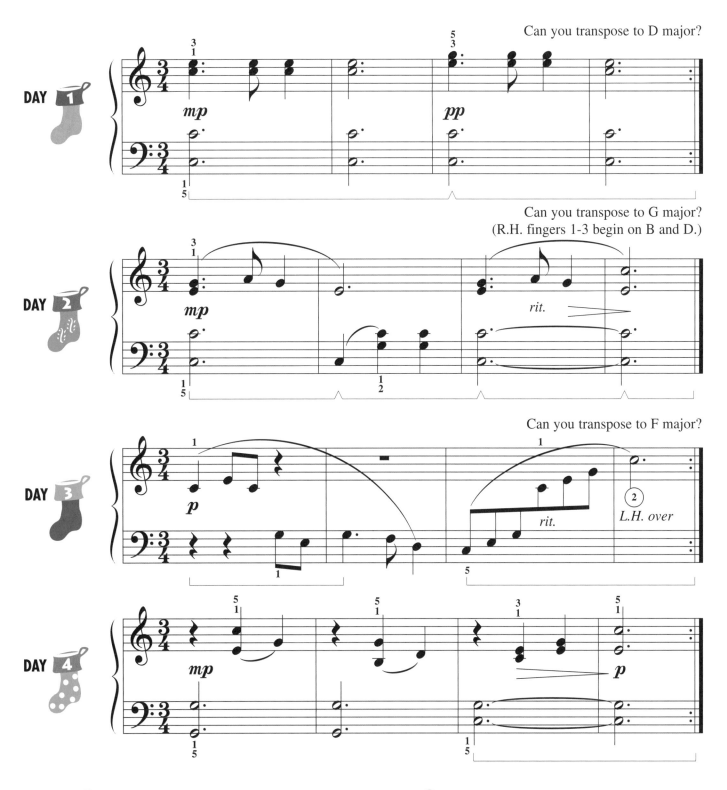

Can you transpose to D major?

DAY 1

Can you transpose to G major?
(R.H. fingers 1-3 begin on B and D.)

DAY 2

Can you transpose to F major?

DAY 3

DAY 4

 DAY 5   In *Silent Night,* circle each left-hand **octave**.

Hint: There are 5.

 DAY 6   In *Silent Night,* put a ✔ above each right-hand **6th**.

Hint: There are 7.

5

Toyland
(the operetta *Babes in Toyland*)

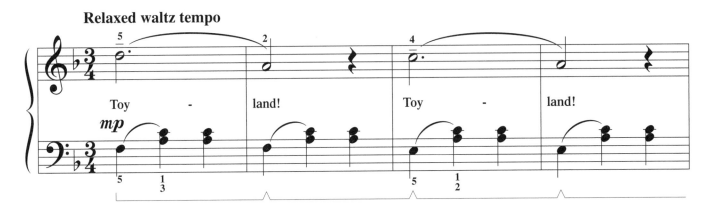

Words by Glen MacDonough
Music by Victor Herbert

Relaxed waltz tempo

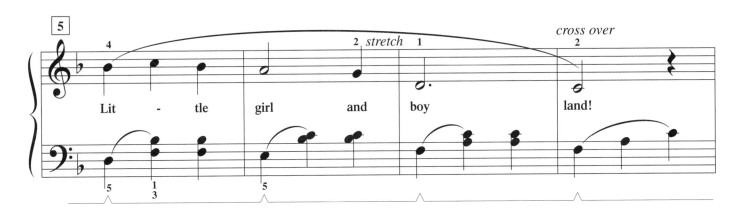

Toy - land! Toy - land!

Lit - tle girl and boy land!

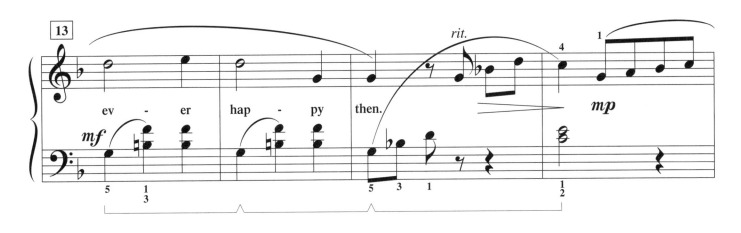

While you dwell with - in it, you are

ev - er hap - py then.

Child - hood's Joy - land,

Mys - tic mer - ry Toy - land!

Once you pass its bor - ders you can

nev - er re - turn a - gain.

TOYLAND STOCKING STUFFERS

("variations" for sightreading)

Sightread one "stocking stuffer" a day while learning *Toyland*.

Circle the stocking after sightreading!

Can you transpose to G major?
(R.H. finger 5 begins on E.)

DAY 1

Can you transpose to C major?
(L.H. finger 1 begins on A.)

DAY 2

Can you transpose to G major?

DAY 3

Hint: Keep eyes moving ahead to prepare each L.H. chord!

DAY 4

DAY 5 Name the correct step of the scale for each note below: **1 2 3 4 5 6** or **7**.

scale step **6**
     Ex.

DAY 6 Put a ✔ above the 3 measures that use a **V7 waltz chord** in F major.

Coventry Carol
(Theme and Variation)

Theme

Traditional English Carol

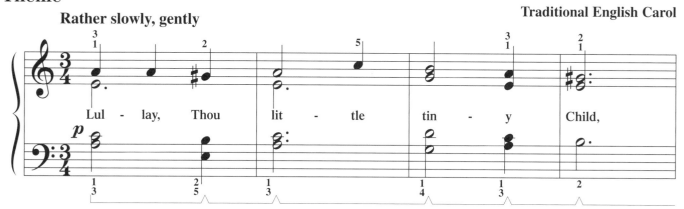

Lul - lay, Thou lit - tle tin - y Child,

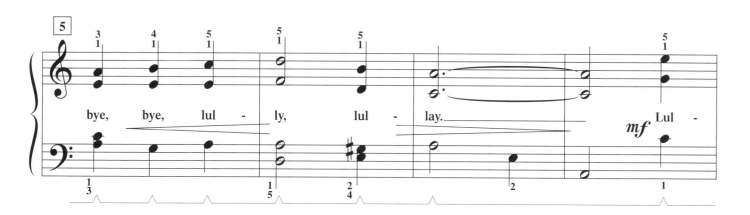

bye, bye, lul - ly, lul - lay. Lul -

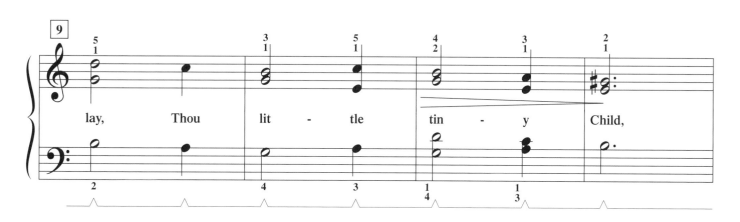

lay, Thou lit - tle tin - y Child,

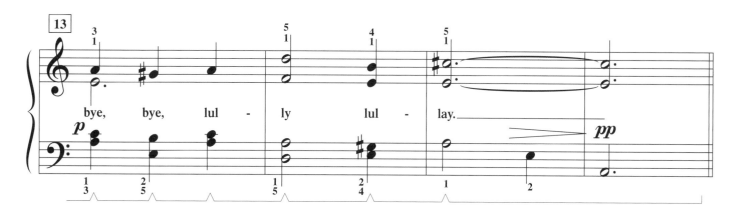

bye, bye, lul - ly lul - lay.

Variation

COVENTRY STOCKING STUFFERS

("variations" for sightreading)

Sightread one "stocking stuffer" a day while learning *Coventry Carol.*

Circle the stocking after sightreading!

Can you transpose to D minor?

The **theme** and **variation** end in A major.

True or False
(circle one)

Can you play the **L.H. alone** of the *theme* while your R.H. taps **beats 1, 2,** and **3** on your lap?

God Rest Ye Merry, Gentlemen

Traditional English Carol

With vigor

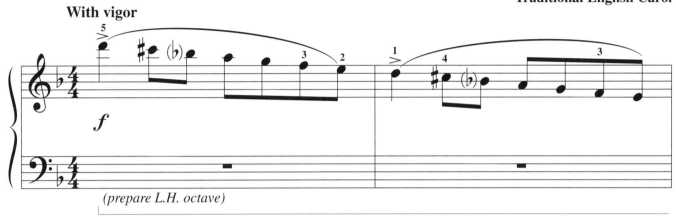

(prepare L.H. octave)

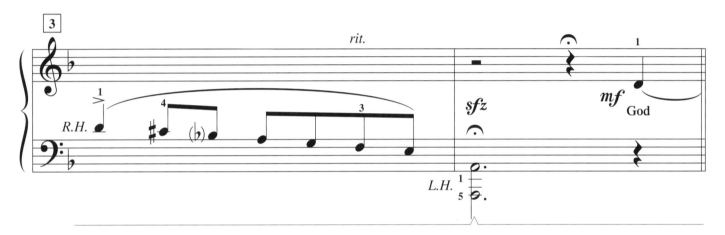

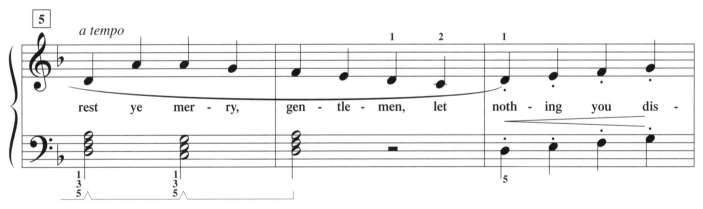

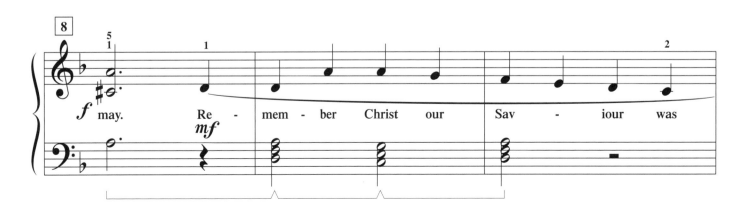

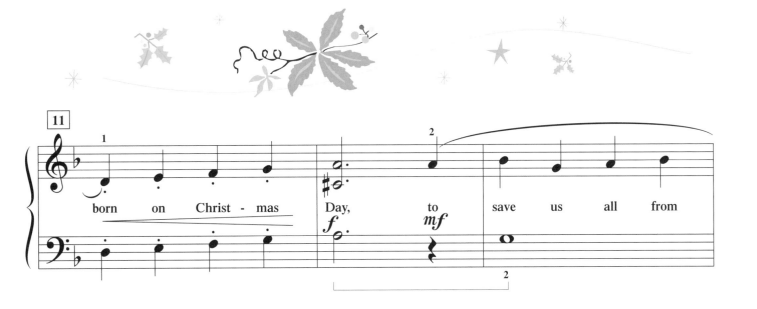

born on Christ - mas Day, to save us all from

Sa - tan's power when we were gone a - stray. O

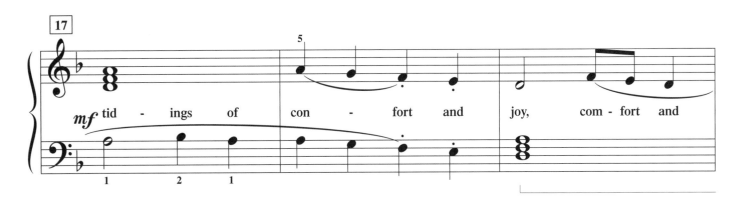

tid - ings of con - fort and joy, com - fort and

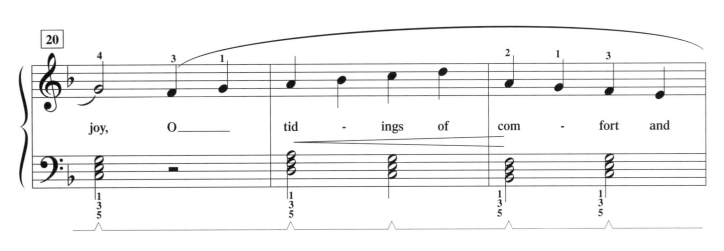

joy, O tid - ings of com - fort and

Sightread one "stocking stuffer" a day
while learning *God Rest Ye Merry, Gentlemen.*

Circle the stocking after sightreading!

("variations" for sightreading)

Can you transpose to A minor?

DAY 1

Can you transpose to A minor?

DAY 2

Can you transpose to A minor?

DAY 3

Can you transpose to A minor?

DAY 4

DAY 5 Is the **C-natural** in *measure 6* from the D natural minor scale or D harmonic minor scale?

(circle one)

DAY 6 Is the **C-sharp** in *measure 8* from the D natural minor scale or D harmonic minor scale?

(circle one)

Joy to the World

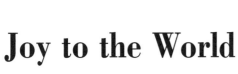

With joy, not too fast

Words by Isaac Watts
Music by George Frideric Handel

Sightread one "stocking stuffer" a day
while learning *Joy to the World*.

Circle the stocking after sightreading!

JOYOUS STOCKING STUFFERS

("variations" for sightreading)

Can you transpose to D major?

DAY 1

f-p on repeat

Can you transpose to G major?

DAY 2

p

Can you transpose to G major?

DAY 3

f

rit.

Can you transpose to F major?

DAY 4

mf

Name the correct step of the scale
for each note below: **1 2 3 4 5 6** or **7**.

DAY 5

scale step 1 (8) ___ ___ ___ ___ ___ ___
Ex.

Put a ✔ above each
measure of the carol
that uses only notes of
the **C major chord**.

DAY 6

Hint: There are 8.

The Twelve Days of Christmas

Rather slow and jazzy (no swing)

Traditional

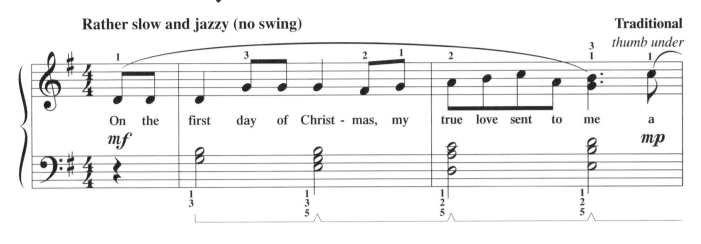

On the first day of Christ-mas, my true love sent to me a

par-tridge___ in a pear tree. On the second day of Christ-mas, my

(prepare L.H.)

true love sent to me two tur-tle doves, and a par-tridge___ in a pear

(prepare L.H.)

tree. On the third day of Christ-mas, my true love sent to me

201

19

Sightread one "stocking stuffer" a day
while learning *The Twelve Days of Christmas.*

Circle the stocking after sightreading!

("variations" for sightreading)

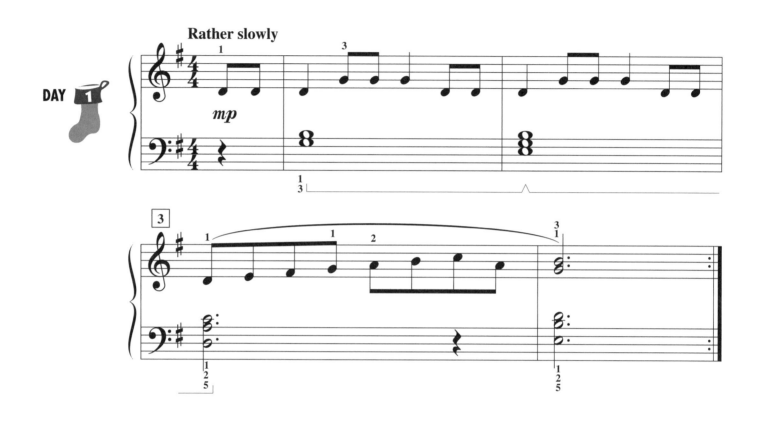

Hint: Watch the R.H. fingering carefully!

FF

What two key signatures are used in this "stocking stuffer?" _____ : 1 flat

_____ : 1 sharp

DAY 3

DAY 4

DAY 5

Circle six **E minor chords** for the L.H. in this piece.

DAY 6

Name the correct step of the scale for each note below: **1 2 3 4 5 6** or **7**.

scale step _5_ __ __ __ __ __ __ __
Ex.

Hallelujah Chorus
(from Handel's *Messiah*)

George Frideric Handel

With joy

24

FF1

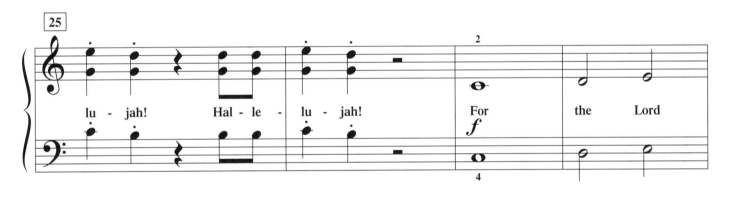

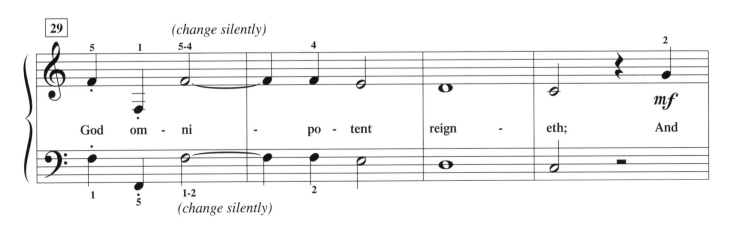

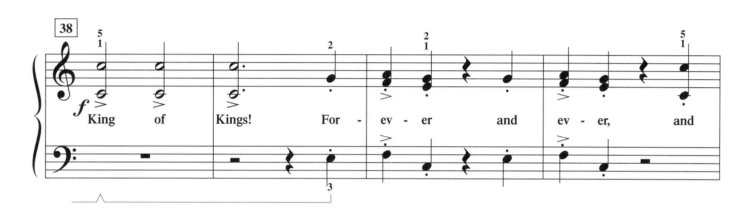

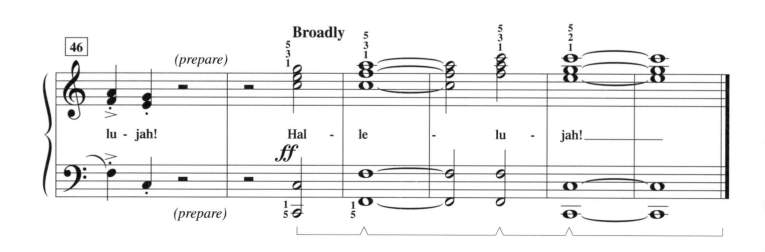

Sightread one "stocking stuffer" a day while learning the *Hallelujah Chorus.*

Circle the stocking after sightreading!

TRIUMPHANT STOCKING STUFFERS

("variations" for sightreading)

First name the intervals in measures 1-2.

rit.

Put a ✔ above each measure with this rhythm:

Hint: There are 9.

Find two places in this piece where the hands play in **parallel motion.**

Parade of the Tin Soldiers

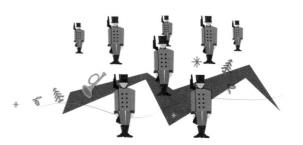

Leon Jessel

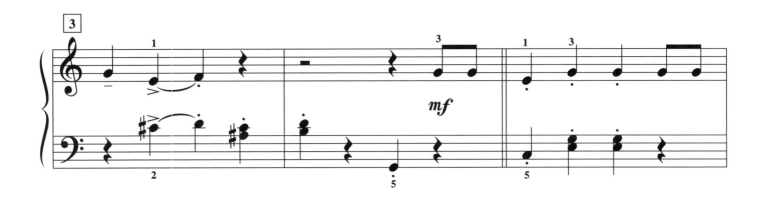

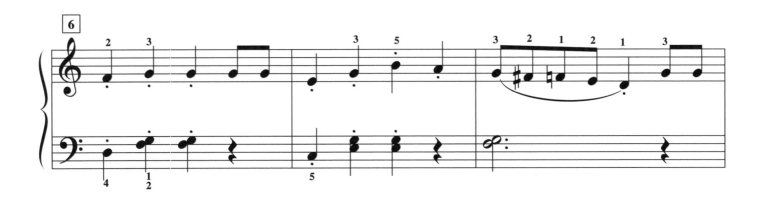

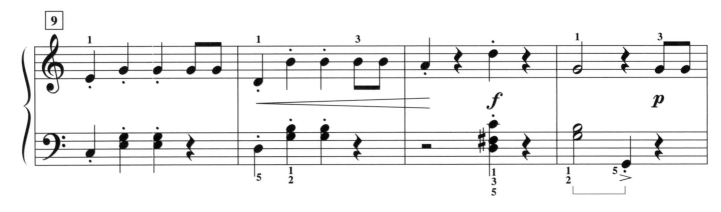

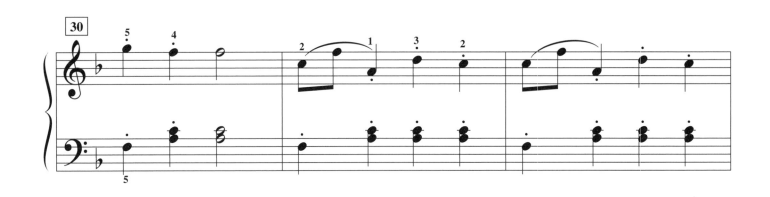

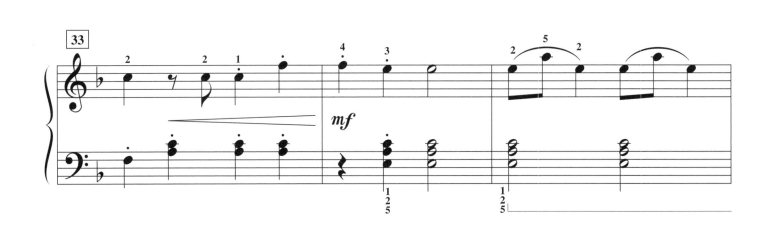

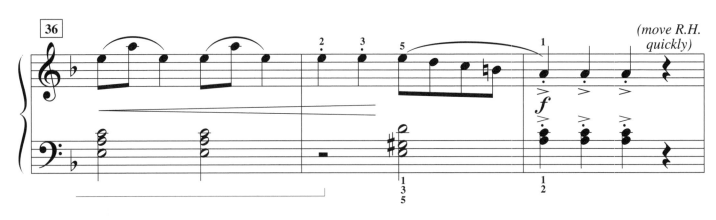

Sightread one "stocking stuffer" a day
while learning *Parade of the Tin Soldiers.*

Circle the stocking after sightreading!

TIN SOLDIER STOCKING STUFFERS

("variations" for sightreading)

DAY 1

DAY 2

DAY 3

DAY 4

DAY 5

Where does *Parade of the Tin Soldiers*
change to a new key? *measure* _____

Write the new key name in the music.

DAY 6

In *measure 8* the R.H. plays a
descending (moving down)
pattern of 8th notes.

Where does the L.H. play an
ascending (moving up) pattern
of 8th notes? *measure* _____